The use of too many  avoided, as it is more encourage comment ~ to expect particular answers.

Care has been taken to retain sufficient realism in the illustrations and subject matter to enable a young child to have fun identifying objects, creatures and situations.

It is wise to remember that patience and understanding are very important, and that children do not all develop evenly or at the same rate. Parents should not be anxious if children do not give correct answers to those questions that are asked. With help, they will do so in their own time.

The brief notes at the back of this book will enable interested parents to make the fullest use of these **Ladybird talkabout** books.

Ladybird Books Loughborough

compiled by W. Murray

illustrated by Harry Wingfield

The publishers wish to acknowledge the assistance of
the nursery school advisers who helped with the
preparation of this book,
especially that of Lady Britton, Chairman,
and Miss M Puddephat, M Ed, Vice Chairman
of The British Association for Early Childhood
Education (formerly The Nursery School Association).

Suggestions for extending the use of this **talkabout** book . . .

The illustrations have been planned to help increase a child's vocabulary and understanding, and the page headings are only brief suggestions as to how these illustrations may be used. For example, you could point out that in the 'Find the pairs' picture there is also **a pair** of socks and **a pair** of hands. You could discuss the colours of the shoes and talk about shoes that are laced and those that are buckled.

There are numerous opportunities for discussion and discovery. When looking at the 'Talk about playing shop' illustration, you could suggest that a child looks for other pictures of the articles (eggs, potatoes, apples, etc.) elsewhere in the book. When looking at the 'Talk about circles' picture, you could suggest looking for wheels on other pages.

With this book a child can be helped to understand various important concepts. For

Talk about
crossing the road

3

1

Tell the story

What will happen next ?

r work ?

Talk about circles

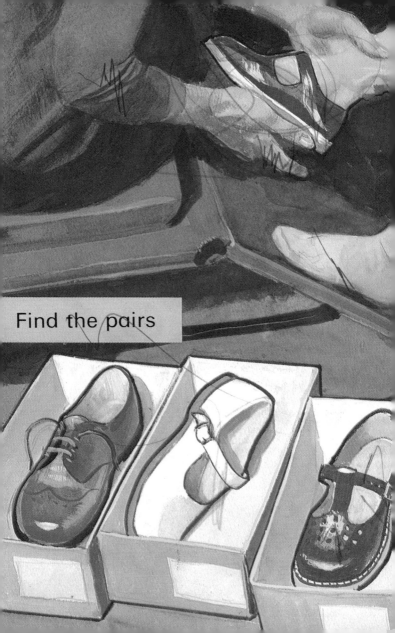

Find the pairs

gether ?

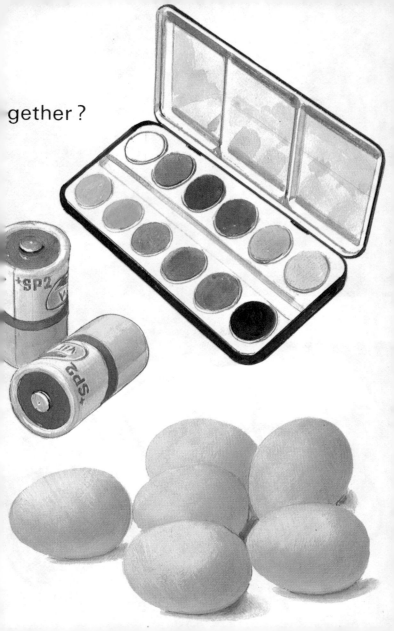

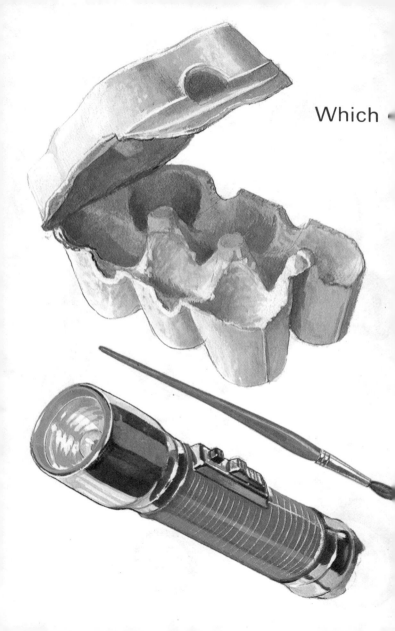

Which

Talk about the toys
How many wheels
on each toy?

Which shall
buy for our
party ?

Talk about playing shop

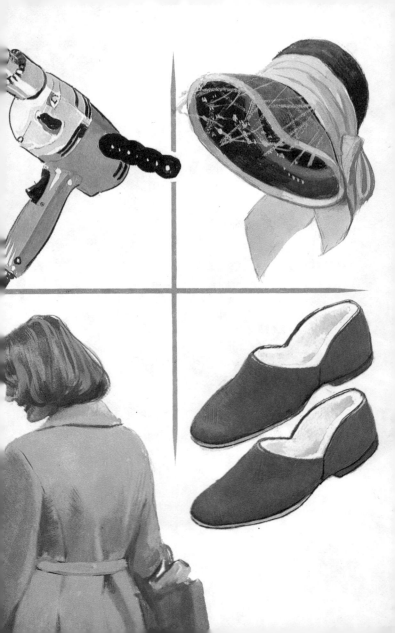

Which shall we
buy to give
Daddy?

all

Talk about long and short, large

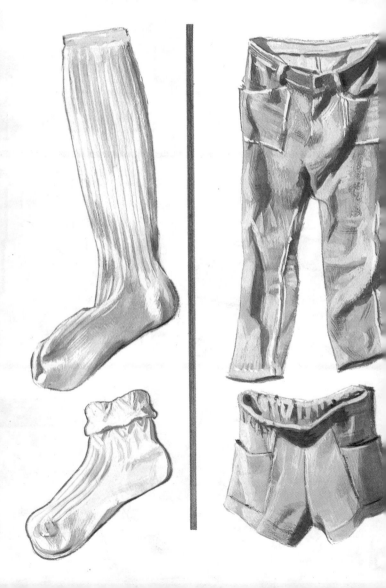

Tell the story

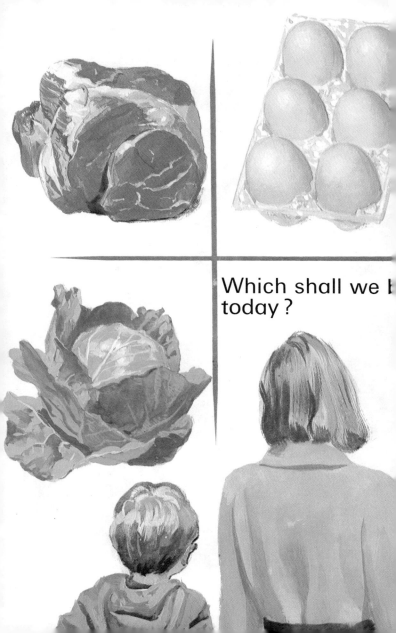

Which shall we b
today?

Tell the story

the pet shop

Talk abo

LOOK and find
another like this

and this

and this

r shopping ?

Which do we u

Tell the story

4

5

6

How many eggs ?

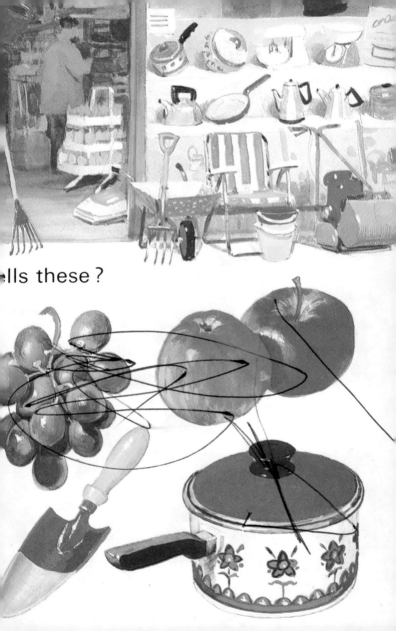

-lls these ?

Which sh

Talk about the colours and shapes

Talk about the pictur

alkabout
shopping